SRA Specific Skill Series
for Reading

Making
Inferences

Sixth Edition

Columbus, OH

The **McGraw·Hill** Companies

SRAonline.com

 **SRA**

Copyright © 2006 by SRA/McGraw-Hill.

Printed in the United States of America.

Send all inquiries to:
SRA/McGraw-Hill
4400 Easton Commons
Columbus, OH 43219

ISBN 0-07-604070-4

3 4 5 6 7 8 9 BCH 12 11 10 09 08

PURPOSE:

MAKING INFERENCES is designed to develop one of the most difficult interpretive skills—arriving at a *probable* conclusion from a limited amount of information. **MAKING INFERENCES** requires students to *read between the lines.* They must utilize previously acquired knowledge and past experiences in order to fully comprehend the message of the text.

FOR WHOM:

The skill of **MAKING INFERENCES** is developed through a series of books spanning ten levels (Picture, Preparatory, A, B, C, D, E, F, G, H). The Picture Level is for students who have not acquired a basic sight vocabulary. The Preparatory Level is for students who have a basic sight vocabulary but are not yet ready for the first-grade-level book. Books A through H are appropriate for students who can read on levels one through eight, respectively.

THE NEW EDITION:

The sixth edition of the *Specific Skill Series for Reading* maintains the quality and focus that has distinguished this program for more than 40 years. A key element central to the program's success has been the unique nature of the reading selections. Fiction and nonfiction pieces about current topics have been designed to stimulate the interest of students, motivating them to use the comprehension strategies they have learned to further their reading. To keep this important aspect of the program intact, a percentage of the reading selections has been replaced in order to ensure the continued relevance of the subject material.

In addition, a significant percentage of the artwork in the program has been replaced to give the books a contemporary look. The cover photographs are designed to appeal to readers of all ages.

SESSIONS:

Short practice sessions are the most effective. It is desirable to have a practice session every day or every other day, using a few units each session.

SCORING:

Students should record their answers on the reproducible worksheets. The worksheets make scoring easier and provide uniform records of the students' work. Using worksheets also avoids consuming the exercise books.

It is important for students to know how well they are doing. For this reason, units should be scored as soon as they have been completed. Then a discussion can be held in which students justify their choices. (The *Language Activity Pages,* many of which are open-ended, do not lend themselves to an objective score; thus there are no answer keys for these pages.)

GENERAL INFORMATION ON *MAKING INFERENCES:*

The difference between a *conclusion* and an *inference,* as presented in this series, is that a conclusion is a logical deduction based upon conclusive evidence, while an inference is an "educated guess" based upon evidence that is less than conclusive. Read this sample:

> Captain Fujihara quickly parked the fire truck, grabbed his helmet, and rushed into the house at 615 Oak Street.

You can *conclude* that Captain Fujihara knows how to drive because that ability was required to park the fire truck. You can *infer* that there is a fire at 615 Oak Street because Captain Fujihara took his helmet and rushed into that house. This is an inference because firefighters do rush to put out fires. It is an inference because there may be another reason for the firefighter's rushing to the house. Captain Fujihara may live there and be late for supper. Thus an inference is supported by evidence, but the evidence is not necessarily conclusive.

SUGGESTED STEPS:

1. Students read the text. After reading, students examine the statements that follow the text to determine whether each is a factually true statement (T), a false statement (F), or a valid inference (I). ("True" statements are those about which the reader can be *certain* from the text.)

2. Then students reexamine the text for evidence to support their decisions.

3. Students record their answers on the worksheets.

RELATED MATERIALS:

Specific Skill Series Assessment Book provides the teacher with a pretest and a posttest for each skill at each grade level. These tests will help the teacher assess the students' performance in each of the nine comprehension skills.

About This Book

In a story a writer does not tell the reader everything. A careful reader is able to make educated guesses about things the author does not tell. An educated guess is a guess that is based on facts the author provides plus the reader's own knowledge and experience. For example, an author may write the following in a story.

> Tara clutched a handkerchief tightly in her fingers. Sobbing, she raised her hand to wipe away the tears that trickled down her cheeks.

You can make an educated guess that Tara is sad, based on the fact that she is crying and on your own knowledge that people sometimes cry when they are sad.

This kind of educated guess is called an **inference.** You cannot be certain that your inference is correct. In the example above, Tara may be crying because she has hurt herself. Or she may be crying because she is very happy. Other details in the story will help you make the best possible guess.

In this book you will read short stories. Then you will read four sentences about each story. You will have to decide whether each sentence is true (T), false (F), or an inference (I). A true statement tells a fact from the story. A false statement is one that is not true. An inference says something that is *probably* true based on facts in the story and your own knowledge and experience. More than one sentence about one story may be true, false, or an inference. You must read each sentence carefully to decide which it is.

1.   Every April when Jamie's school celebrates Earth Day, students receive a blue spruce sapling to plant. Jamie plants her trees along the border of their yard. When she was younger, she forgot to water her trees and they died. But each tree from the last four years has survived, and her family now has a nice row of blue spruces growing along the side of their yard.

2.   "You're never going to make it up that hill, Bob, without a ten-speed bike like mine," said Kim.

      "You may be right, Kim, but I'm certainly going to try," answered Bob. By the time Bob got halfway up the hill, he was breathing hard and his legs were getting tired of pedaling. Finally he got off the bike and walked with it up the last part of the hill.

      "I knew this old bike would make it," he said with a laugh, as he reached the top.

3.   "Do you know that crayfish shed their shells?" Carlos asked his friends. "Yesterday when I was eating my cereal, I saw my crayfish huddled in the corner of its tank. I thought it was sick, and I started getting worried. When I came home from school, he looked bigger and darker. Then I found what looked like his old, empty shell lying on the bottom of his tank."

4.   Su-Lin is a star soccer player on her team. During the first four games of the season, she scored at least two goals in each game. Yesterday she twisted her ankle and had to sit out for the rest of the game. Her team lost. They have another game scheduled tomorrow. Su-Lin's coach doesn't know if she is ready to play even though Su-Lin said her ankle feels better.

5.   "Well, now we will see if my time machine really works, Rahan," said Dr. Anthony, closing the door on the familiar twenty-first century.

      "If I remember correctly, we will not be aware of any time passing at all," remarked Rahan.

      "That's right," the doctor responded. "We should be able to open the door right about now and look out on Earth in very ancient times. Let's try it out, Rahan."

      Opening the door, Dr. Anthony gasped. "It worked, Rahan! I do believe that is a dinosaur we see grazing over there!"

		T	F	I
1.	(A) Jamie forgot to plant her Earth Day tree some years.	☐	☐	☐
	(B) Jamie's family has at least four blue spruces growing in their yard.	☐	☐	☐
	(C) Earth Day is in April.	☐	☐	☐
	(D) Now that Jamie is older, she is more responsible about watering.	☐	☐	☐

		T	F	I
2.	(A) Bob walked his bike up the last part of the hill.	☐	☐	☐
	(B) Bob isn't a person who quits without making an effort.	☐	☐	☐
	(C) Bob had a brand-new bike.	☐	☐	☐
	(D) Kim was proud to own a ten-speed bike.	☐	☐	☐

		T	F	I
3.	(A) Carlos's pet crayfish lives in a tank.	☐	☐	☐
	(B) Crayfish shed their shells when they grow.	☐	☐	☐
	(C) Carlos's crayfish shed its shell while he was away at school.	☐	☐	☐
	(D) The crayfish was ill.	☐	☐	☐

		T	F	I
4.	(A) Su-Lin has an ankle injury.	☐	☐	☐
	(B) Su-Lin's team depends on her to score goals that help them win.	☐	☐	☐
	(C) The coach makes his players play the day after an injury.	☐	☐	☐
	(D) Su-Lin scored at least eight goals so far this season.	☐	☐	☐

		T	F	I
5.	(A) At first Dr. Anthony was unsure that the time machine would really work.	☐	☐	☐
	(B) Dr. Anthony closed the door on the twenty-first century.	☐	☐	☐
	(C) Dr. Anthony expected to open the door and look out on Earth in ancient times.	☐	☐	☐
	(D) The two time travelers have landed in prehistoric times.	☐	☐	☐

1. Rasheed was excited when he heard about a chess club that had recently formed at the YMCA. He had played chess for three years and could beat everyone in his family. Most games were over in less than 15 minutes. His friend Jason said that anyone age 12 and older could play at the YMCA club. He'd played last week against an adult who had some very tough moves.

2. "I'm planning to keep a journal in the new year," Josh told Tara. "Is it hard work?"

    "Not really," replied Tara. "Most people enjoy talking to themselves through their writing. A journal is a real help to the memory too. You can always refer to it to verify a date."

    "What are some suggestions for someone just starting to keep a diary?" asked Josh.

    "The important thing is to get your thoughts and feelings on paper without wasting a lot of time. Try to include both the good and bad happenings and how they affect you," advised Tara.

3. Kaitlin tried to breathe calmly through her snorkel and rest at the water's surface. Other snorkelers who were swimming nearby said a group of stingrays was passing through the lagoon. She wanted to see them, but every time she looked down, her heart began to race when she saw what she thought was a barracuda. When she saw a silver flash, she quickly reversed her direction.

4. Just as Alex thought his group had conquered the summit of Mt. Majestic, he looked up and saw one more peak. The sun was going down, and he knew that he should lead his five climbers back down the mountain, even though they might not like it. It would be dark in three hours. Last week on a descent two climbers fell over loose rocks and were injured.

5. The mural had to be finished in two weeks, so the painters began working later every day. Soon it would be Phoenixville's 150th anniversary. The whole town was getting ready for its sesquicentennial. After a morning of festivities, a parade through the old steel town would end at the park, where people would be able to enjoy the newly painted scene of a phoenix bird flying over the steel mill.

Unit 2

1. (A) Rasheed had recently learned to play chess.   T F I
   (B) People age 12 and older played chess at the YMCA.
   (C) Rasheed was eager to be challenged by other chess players.
   (D) People had to be the same age to play chess against each other at the club.

2. (A) Josh plans to start a journal.   T F I
   (B) Tara has had experience in keeping a journal.
   (C) Tara advised writing only good events in the journal.
   (D) Tara said people talk to themselves through their writing.

3. (A) Kaitlin wanted to see the stingrays.   T F I
   (B) Barracudas made Kaitlin nervous.
   (C) Kaitlin kept losing her snorkel.
   (D) Other snorkelers saw the stingrays.

4. (A) The sun had disappeared behind clouds.   T F I
   (B) It would be unsafe to descend the mountain in the dark.
   (C) Alex was the leader of five other climbers.
   (D) The group was climbing Mt. Pleasant.

5. (A) Steel was once manufactured in Phoenixville.   T F I
   (B) The phoenix was a symbol for the town of Phoenixville.
   (C) Phoenixville planned to celebrate its 100th anniversary.
   (D) The new mural was a central part of the celebration.

1.   "I'm very worried about my grade on this science test," Nick said glumly. He shook his head slowly back and forth. "I hope I passed."

    When Nick had left, Molly remarked to Allison, "Nick says how worried he is, yet he always gets excellent grades."

    "Yes, I've noticed that too," said Allison. "He likes to get attention. He pretends to be really worried about tests that he knows he got an 'A' on."

    "He got a perfect score in math last week, but he had told everyone he was sure that he had failed," said Molly. "When he only got a 70 percent the week before, though, he didn't say a word."

2.   "This road is in terrible condition," said Mom. The car hit another bump.

    "Yes," agreed Dad. "It's just full of potholes. How are you holding up with the driving?"

    "Oh, I'm all right," answered Mom. "Are you kids getting carsick?" she asked as she looked into the rearview mirror.

    "Yes!" moaned the two children at the same time.

    "Then I'll slow down even more," said Mom. "Imagine paying a toll to drive on a road at this speed! I wonder where all the money goes."

3.   "Hey, do you want to play?" called Adam.

    The boy Adam was speaking to had been kicking a soccer ball across the grass. "Play what?" he asked.

    "Football," answered Adam. "We need another player."

    "I sure do!" answered the boy. "We play a lot of *fútbol* in my country." He smiled briefly. "I'm from Spain. My name is Carlos. We can use my ball if you like."

    "But that's a soccer ball," said Adam doubtfully.

    "Oh, of course," laughed the boy. "You play American football. I've never played it before, but I'd like to give it a try."

4.   Hawaiian islanders are no strangers to volcanoes. The whole island chain was formed by volcanic action long ago. Tourists put the volcanoes and their craters high on their "must see" lists. Carloads and busloads of visitors climb the winding roads to the tops of volcanoes, especially if they are active volcanoes. Kilauea, located in Hawaii Volcanoes National Park, has a large parking lot at its highest point.

5.   Hawaii's famous Mauna Loa is the world's biggest volcano. It looms 13,680 feet above the ocean and extends 16,000 feet below the sea, for a total height of more than 29,000 feet. Half the island of Hawaii is covered with old lava flows from this volcano. When Mauna Loa starts rumbling, residents of Hilo, the nearest city, do not panic. They know that the lava will flow slowly enough for them to evacuate in time.

		T	F	I
1.	(A) Nick always got poor grades.	☐	☐	☐
	(B) Molly and Allison discussed Nick's reactions to tests.	☐	☐	☐
	(C) Allison said that Nick likes to get attention.	☐	☐	☐
	(D) Allison and Molly know Nick better than he realizes they do.	☐	☐	☐

		T	F	I
2.	(A) The bumping over potholes didn't bother the children.	☐	☐	☐
	(B) The money collected at toll booths covers the costs of road repairs.	☐	☐	☐
	(C) Dad asked the children if they wanted to get out and walk.	☐	☐	☐
	(D) There were two children in the car.	☐	☐	☐

		T	F	I
3.	(A) The Spanish play *fútbol* with a soccer ball.	☐	☐	☐
	(B) Carlos had played American football before.	☐	☐	☐
	(C) Adam asked Carlos to play football.	☐	☐	☐
	(D) Carlos had been kicking a soccer ball across the grass.	☐	☐	☐

		T	F	I
4.	(A) Tourists in Hawaii are not permitted on the summits of volcanoes.	☐	☐	☐
	(B) The Hawaiian Islands were formed by volcanoes.	☐	☐	☐
	(C) The tourists like a little excitement as long as there is no real danger.	☐	☐	☐
	(D) Kilauea is located in Hawaii Volcanoes National Park.	☐	☐	☐

		T	F	I
5.	(A) Hilo's residents have experienced previous lava flows.	☐	☐	☐
	(B) Mauna Loa is the largest volcano in the world.	☐	☐	☐
	(C) Hilo's residents live in fear of Mauna Loa.	☐	☐	☐
	(D) Mauna Loa has erupted before.	☐	☐	☐

1.　　"I'll pay the three of you 15 dollars to dig the hole for a tree in my backyard," said Mrs. Martin as she gave Beth, David, and Andrew each a shovel.

　　All three began to dig. Soon Andrew said, "I'm going home to get a drink. I'll be back in five minutes." He didn't return until the hole was almost dug.

　　When the hole was finished, Mrs. Martin said, "Here are the 15 dollars I owe you, but I'm not going to divide it evenly because one of you didn't do as much work."

　　Beth and David got six dollars each; Andrew got only three.

2.　　Simon braced his leg against the starting block. "I've got to win this race," he breathed. He thought about what his grandfather had told him.

　　"It doesn't matter what you do in life," his grandfather had said. "Just make sure you do the best job you can."

　　The starting gun went off. Simon forged ahead at the beginning of the race. When he crossed the finish line, Simon knew he had won easily. What he didn't know was that he had also broken the school record.

3.　　"Have you ever ridden a tandem bicycle?" asked Claire.

　　"No. Are they the bikes with two seats?" asked Ashish.

　　"Yes. The front person controls the steering and brakes. It is hard to balance at first, and the bike feels heavy, but once you get going it's really fun for both riders. You do have to work together, though."

　　"It sounds like fun. I'd like to try it," said Ashish.

4.　　Some birds such as ostriches cannot even fly. Ostriches do have another talent, however. To escape from lions and other predators, ostriches use their long legs and sturdy feet to run at speeds well over 45 miles an hour. While searching for vegetation to eat, their great speed also helps them cover the vast plains of southern Africa where they live. Ostriches are the fastest birds on foot.

5.　　"It's never been so cold," said Pedro. "Not that I can remember."

　　"If you think it's cold now," warned Mr. Suthard, "just wait. The forecast says the temperature tonight will drop to 10 degrees below zero."

　　"I'd rather be living at the North Pole," complained Pedro. "I can't wait for summer!"

　　"And when summer comes, you'll wish it were winter again," answered his neighbor, Mr. Suthard.

		T	F	I

1. **(A)** Andrew didn't get paid as much as Beth and David.

(B) Mrs. Martin was looking out her back window while the children were digging.

(C) David ran home for a shovel.

(D) Andrew didn't do as much work as his friends.

2. **(A)** Simon remembered what his grandfather had told him.

(B) What Simon's grandfather had told him made Simon do his best job.

(C) Simon's grandfather would be happy to know how hard Simon tried.

(D) Simon was behind in the beginning of the race.

3. **(A)** Ashish has no interest in tandem bicycles.

(B) Claire has experience riding a tandem bicycle.

(C) It takes practice to learn to ride a tandem bicycle.

(D) The riders on a tandem bicycle must work together.

4. **(A)** Ostriches are not the only birds that cannot fly.

(B) Ostriches are meat eaters.

(C) Lions prey on ostriches.

(D) Ostriches use their speed to survive.

5. **(A)** Mr. Suthard told Pedro the weather forecast for that night.

(B) The temperature was not expected to get any colder.

(C) Mr. Suthard was Pedro's neighbor.

(D) Pedro often complains about the weather.

1.   Mr. Davis noticed a fresh, slick stain on the floor of his garage, right where the front of his car usually stops. "Oh, no," he thought. "Something's leaking from my car." He bent down and sniffed the stain. "It doesn't smell like oil." He checked the water in the radiator and the brake fluid. "They are both full. No leaks there. I don't have power steering or air-conditioning, and my windshield-washer-fluid container has been empty for a month. There are no other possibilities. It's a mystery."

2.   "I need to find a green Eagles shirt, brown corduroy pants, and a baseball cap," said Tyler.

    "Why? What's going on?" asked his mother.

    "It's spirit week at school this week, and tomorrow is twin day. That's what Brian and I decided on today at school."

    "Well you have the cap, you can borrow one of Greg's Eagles shirts, and I'll wash your brown corduroy pants," suggested his mother.

3.   "We're out of eggs, Sis," Willis complained. "We can't make supper."

    "I was afraid we might be," declared Sis. "In this cold weather, Mom usually stops at the Hope Diner on her way home from work for a cup of hot tea. The waiter knows her. Let's call the diner and leave a message for her." Sis dialed the diner.

    An hour later Mom came in with a bag of groceries but no eggs.

4.   The Coopers did not want to cut down their giant cherry tree, but the arborist told them it was diseased. As they stood looking at its cut trunk, they counted more than 300 light and dark rings. "The tree must have been really old," said Kendra. "The thicker, light rings came from growth that happens in spring and summer, and the darker, narrow rings are from the slower fall and winter growth."

5.   Kim was delighted to visit her cousin in Mexico, but she hadn't expected such hot weather. "I really can't stand this heat," she confided to her cousin.

    "Tomorrow will be better," her cousin assured her. "I've arranged for us to swim in our neighbor's outdoor pool."

    "Oh boy!" shouted Kim. "A plunge into cold, refreshing water. I can't wait!"

    "Don't get your hopes up too high," sighed her cousin.

	T	F	I
1. **(A)** Mr. Davis considered six possibilities for the leak.	☐	☐	☐
(B) Mr. Davis will ask a mechanic to solve the mystery.	☐	☐	☐
(C) The liquid stain smelled like oil.	☐	☐	☐
(D) Mr. Davis solved the mystery.	☐	☐	☐

	T	F	I
2. **(A)** Tyler does not own any of the items he needs for twin day.	☐	☐	☐
(B) Brian and Tyler are biological twins.	☐	☐	☐
(C) Brian has access to the same clothing items that Tyler plans to wear.	☐	☐	☐
(D) Twin day is a part of spirit week.	☐	☐	☐

	T	F	I
3. **(A)** Mom had gone shopping instead of stopping at the diner for tea.	☐	☐	☐
(B) Willis discovered that there were no eggs in the house.	☐	☐	☐
(C) Mom had a dozen eggs in her bag of groceries.	☐	☐	☐
(D) Sis decided to call the diner and leave a message.	☐	☐	☐

	T	F	I
4. **(A)** The Coopers' cherry tree had a disease.	☐	☐	☐
(B) Cherry trees do not grow in fall and winter.	☐	☐	☐
(C) The Cooper's cherry tree was at least 150 years old.	☐	☐	☐
(D) A tree expert had recommended cutting down the tree.	☐	☐	☐

	T	F	I
5. **(A)** The pool water would not be cool.	☐	☐	☐
(B) The neighbors had an indoor pool.	☐	☐	☐
(C) Kim had not expected Mexico to be so hot.	☐	☐	☐
(D) Kim did not enjoy visiting her cousin.	☐	☐	☐

1.   Emma waited for her turn to read her poem in front of the class. *This is a pretty good poem,* she thought to herself. *It's just that. . . .* Then her name was called, she stood up, and her knees began to shake. When she turned around and looked at the rest of the class, however, she saw friendly faces. *Maybe this won't be so bad after all,* Emma thought with relief.

2.   As the ecology class traipsed through the woods, Ms. Liem pointed out the mosses and ferns native to the biome. She also warned the students to stay away from the many patches of native three-leaf plants—poison ivy. Mariah thought of her sister, who was highly allergic to poison ivy, but Mariah didn't seem especially concerned. Some of it even brushed against her ankles. The other students carefully watched their step.

3.   Justin was frustrated. He was never able to use the computer. His older sister was constantly e-mailing her friends, and his brother needed it for long stretches of time to do research and write term papers. His parents had their own computer that was off-limits to the rest of the family. He had an idea. What if he woke up early, before the rest of the family?

4.   "Look at our new puppy. Isn't he cute? We've named him Snowball," Craig said. "He needs to have puppy shots, though, and we don't know which doctor to take him to. Can you recommend a good vet?"

    "Of course!" his neighbor answered. "We always go to Dr. Lina Cruz. She was just terrific when Patches was so sick last summer. She identified the problem right away, and Patches was healthy and purring again within just a few days."

5.   The sun beamed down on the sweltering city streets. Carl and Evan moped along, sweating. "We've got to beat this heat," groaned Carl.

    "Let's take the bus to the beach," suggested Evan.

    "Neither one of us has enough money for the bus," said Carl. "We can't afford an air-conditioned movie, either."

    "I know," cried Evan. "Let's go read at the library."

    "Great idea!" responded Carl, and they ran off.

1.   T F I

1. **(A)** Emma went to the back of the room. ☐ ☐ ☐
   (B) Emma was afraid of speaking in front of the class. ☐ ☐ ☐
   (C) As soon as Emma stood up, she felt calm. ☐ ☐ ☐
   (D) The faces of her classmates were friendly. ☐ ☐ ☐

                                                    T F I

2. **(A)** Mariah did not recognize the poison ivy. ☐ ☐ ☐
   (B) Mariah has never had a serious reaction to poison ivy. ☐ ☐ ☐
   (C) Poison ivy is an alien species. ☐ ☐ ☐
   (D) The woods had native ferns and mosses. ☐ ☐ ☐

                                                    T F I

3. **(A)** Justin's brother used the computer to play computer games. ☐ ☐ ☐
   (B) Justin's family had two computers that were in use. ☐ ☐ ☐
   (C) Justin hoped to find computer time early in the morning. ☐ ☐ ☐
   (D) Justin had limited computer access. ☐ ☐ ☐

                                                    T F I

4. **(A)** Craig asked his neighbor to recommend a good vet. ☐ ☐ ☐
   (B) Patches is the neighbor's pet cat. ☐ ☐ ☐
   (C) The name of Craig's new puppy is Snowball. ☐ ☐ ☐
   (D) Patches is always healthy. ☐ ☐ ☐

                                                    T F I

5. **(A)** Carl suggested going to the beach. ☐ ☐ ☐
   (B) The library is a cool place. ☐ ☐ ☐
   (C) The boys could not afford the bus or the movies. ☐ ☐ ☐
   (D) They will not have to spend money at the library. ☐ ☐ ☐

"It's never been so cold," said Pedro. "Not that I can remember."

"If you think it's cold now," warned Mr. Suthard, "just wait. The forecast says the temperature tonight will drop to 10 degrees below zero."

"I'd rather be living at the North Pole," complained Pedro. "I can't wait for summer!"

"And when summer comes, you'll wish it were winter again," answered his neighbor, Mr. Suthard.

A. Exercising Your Skill

In the passage above, two neighbors are talking about the weather. In your reading you may come across stories in which the seasons and weather will be part of the setting. The weather can affect the characters, the events, and the way things turn out at the end of the story. Sometimes an author will directly state what the season or weather is and how the characters feel about it. At other times, you can figure out the season or weather by reading "between the lines" for clues.

Write the four words below as headings on your paper. Under each heading, write words or phrases that make you think about that season. To your list, add some words that tell how people feel at that time of the year or what they do. For example, under Summer, you might first write: *hot, sunny, vacation time.* Then you might write: *go to the beach, cook outdoors, drink lemonade.*

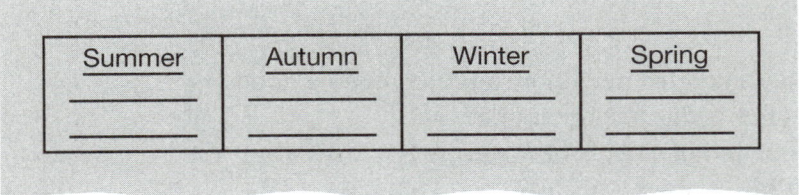

Summer	Autumn	Winter	Spring
_____	_____	_____	_____
_____	_____	_____	_____

B. Expanding Your Skill

With a partner, play this game. Take turns reading the sentence starters below to each other. Have your partner finish each sentence.

1. In hot weather I usually wear _____.

2. In hot weather I like to eat _____.

3. In hot weather I like to play _____.

4. In hot weather I like to go to _____.

5. In hot weather I often feel _____.

C. Exploring Language

Read the sentences below. Choose one of them to be the main idea for your own short story. Describe just how the weather makes your story character feel. Choose words that paint a picture, like *chilled to the bone*. Write your story. Then share what you wrote with your classmates. Ask them to describe how the weather makes the character feel. Ask them to identify the details—stated and unstated—that helped them figure out the character's feelings.

Story Ideas:

- As soon as Julia arrived at camp, she wanted to jump into the pool.
- Ben sniffled as he dragged the rake through layers of dry, fallen leaves.
- Emily pulled her wool scarf up around her red nose and stuffed her hands deep into her coat pockets.
- Seichi hummed, taking a deep breath of the warm, fresh air and listening to the robins chirp.
- Juan held his kite high as he ran across the field on that windy day.

You may want to use the questions below to help you organize your story:

- Who is the main character?
- Where does the story take place?
- What is the weather like, and how does it affect the main character?
- What problem, if any, does the main character face?
- How does he or she try to solve that problem?
- How does the story end?

D. Expressing Yourself

Choose one of these activities.

1. Think of a story that you have read or have seen on television in which the action included a thunderstorm, blizzard, heat wave, or other extreme weather. Give a summary of the story, but leave out the ending. Have your classmates use the clues you gave to figure out the ending.

2. Mimes are people who communicate without words. They pantomime, or act out, ideas using facial expressions and body movements. With a partner, practice using your faces and bodies to describe someone on a very cold or a very hot day. Then present your pantomime to your classmates, and see if they can guess what kind of weather it is.

1. "Jennifer, I would really like you to consider switching to tenor saxophone. We already have plenty of alto saxophones but no tenors. I even have an extra one you could borrow," said Mr. Bonnard. "I know you would pick it up quickly."

    "I hear the parts are not as interesting for tenor. Is that true?" replied Jennifer.

    "When you become advanced, they are even more interesting," said Mr. Bonnard.

    "Hmm," responded Jennifer thoughtfully.

2. Shivering is not the most pleasant sensation, but it does serve a practical purpose. Shivering is the body's own way of creating heat. When a person feels cold, the brain sends messages to very small muscles under the skin. The muscles begin to move rapidly, causing the person who is cold to shiver. The rapid shaking of these muscles actually releases heat that raises the body's surface temperature.

3. The world's largest jellyfish has 1,200 deadly tentacles, some of which are 200 feet long. This ocean creature can grow up to eight feet across and three feet thick. It is found only in the icy waters of the Arctic Ocean. It floats along with its tentacles trailing in the water. Any creature—fish or shellfish—that gets entangled is stung by the hundreds of tentacles that touch it. The creature thrashes and suffers until the jellyfish contracts its tentacles to bring the victim up to its mouth.

4. "I'll boil these eggs and devil them for our picnic," said Brian.

    "Good idea," said Aunt Ruth, "but I'd get rid of the one egg that's floating. It's probably not fresh."

    "That's right," replied Brian. "Fresh eggs sink, and rotten eggs float. I'd almost forgotten about that from our science class."

    "I think it's because that as time passes, pressure from gases builds up inside the egg and pushes out water," volunteered Aunt Ruth.

    "That makes sense," said Brian, "but I wonder why people eat 100-year-old eggs and consider them delicacies."

    "Those aren't rotten! They're pickled," laughed Aunt Ruth. "They're just called 100-year eggs, but they aren't really."

5. King penguins are clever creatures! Living in the cold, dry lands of Antarctica, they are unable to find enough nesting material to protect their newly laid eggs. The King species, therefore, takes matters into its own hands, or onto its own feet. Penguin parents take turns resting a new egg on their feet and warming it with their belly folds. After the egg is hatched, the penguin parents continue to act as foot-nests until the baby penguin is large enough to withstand the Antarctic climate.

Unit 7

		T	F	I
1.	(A) Jennifer currently plays alto saxophone.	☐	☐	☐
	(B) Mr. Bonnard believed Jennifer was musically versatile.	☐	☐	☐
	(C) Jennifer would consider Mr. Bonnard's proposal.	☐	☐	☐
	(D) Jennifer heard that the parts for the tenor saxophone were more interesting.	☐	☐	☐

		T	F	I
2.	(A) The writer thinks people like to shiver.	☐	☐	☐
	(B) The brain responds to changes in the body's surface temperature.	☐	☐	☐
	(C) Shivering is the main way people keep warm.	☐	☐	☐
	(D) Small muscles lie under the skin.	☐	☐	☐

		T	F	I
3.	(A) Any creature caught in the jellyfish's tentacles gets stung.	☐	☐	☐
	(B) The tentacles of the jellyfish contain a poison that can harm or kill.	☐	☐	☐
	(C) The world's largest jellyfish lives in the Pacific Ocean.	☐	☐	☐
	(D) Some of the jellyfish's tentacles are 200 feet long.	☐	☐	☐

		T	F	I
4.	(A) Aunt Ruth said that as time passes, water escapes from an egg and makes it lighter.	☐	☐	☐
	(B) Brian likes deviled eggs.	☐	☐	☐
	(C) Brian was going to make scrambled eggs for the picnic.	☐	☐	☐
	(D) Aunt Ruth said the egg that was floating was probably not fresh.	☐	☐	☐

		T	F	I
5.	(A) New penguin eggs are very fragile.	☐	☐	☐
	(B) King penguins are clever birds.	☐	☐	☐
	(C) Penguin fathers help care for the young.	☐	☐	☐
	(D) Penguins live in warm climates.	☐	☐	☐

1.   Abby and Tony put the last dishes away together. "The kitchen looks great, Abby!" Tony said. There was still a lot of work to do, though. Abby began to make beds and then cleaned her room. Tony started to vacuum the carpets. After finishing that job, he cleaned his room.

Earlier that morning, both of them had made a list. Now they stopped to check off the completed jobs. "Good," Abby said. "We can finish the house before Mom gets home."

2.   Luis looked down at the swirling motion of the skaters. The ice was jammed with old and young; age did not matter here. To Luis, everyone seemed to be racing along the surface madly. He couldn't imagine where he, a newcomer to this sport, could find room to try out his new skates. "Christina," he asked in a small voice, "do you think we could come back when there are fewer skaters?"

"Don't be silly," his friend Christina replied. "Once you get on the ice, you'll forget all about the crowds."

3.   David was surprised to see the middle school lunch menu. He knew that the middle school cafeteria used the same food service as did his elementary school, and he was expecting the same old hamburgers, hot dogs, and chicken nuggets. Instead he was pleased to see teriyaki beef and broccoli pizza, Asian spicy chicken, and avocado turkey wraps on the menu. He just might look into buying a meal ticket.

4.   Gabriella's mother told her that if she raked all the leaves in their yard over the weekend she could earn 15 dollars. Gabriella ended up going shopping on Saturday with her friend and staying at her house overnight. On Sunday she had an all-day swim meet. She planned to rake the leaves on Monday after school, but when she arrived home, she saw the leaves neatly raked into piles.

5.   As the small bat flew haphazardly through the house, Ben looked for a tennis racket to swat it. Sara remembered learning why it is important to protect bats. They eat hundreds of insects, including mosquitoes, every evening. She also remembered hearing about bats' echolocation, which is their ability to use sound and their large ears to "hear" objects and openings. She and Ben opened their living room windows and watched hopefully while the bat circled.

	T	**F**	**I**
1. (A) Tony was pleased with the appearance of the kitchen.	☐	☐	☐
(B) Tony would clean Abby's room.	☐	☐	☐
(C) Abby started to vacuum the carpets.	☐	☐	☐
(D) Abby and Tony wanted to surprise their mom with a clean house.	☐	☐	☐

	T	**F**	**I**
2. (A) There were few people on the ice.	☐	☐	☐
(B) Christina had been skating before.	☐	☐	☐
(C) Luis wanted to skate at another time.	☐	☐	☐
(D) Christina didn't want to miss a chance to skate.	☐	☐	☐

	T	**F**	**I**
3. (A) David is an adventurous eater.	☐	☐	☐
(B) While in elementary school, David did not often buy a meal ticket.	☐	☐	☐
(C) The menu was the same as it had been in elementary school.	☐	☐	☐
(D) The middle school and elementary school used the same food service.	☐	☐	☐

	T	**F**	**I**
4. (A) Gabriella spent her 15 dollars shopping.	☐	☐	☐
(B) Gabriella could earn 15 dollars by raking leaves.	☐	☐	☐
(C) Gabriella's mother had raked the leaves.	☐	☐	☐
(D) Gabriella lost her chance to earn the 15 dollars.	☐	☐	☐

	T	**F**	**I**
5. (A) Bats use their large eyes to navigate.	☐	☐	☐
(B) Bats eat mosquitoes.	☐	☐	☐
(C) Ben wanted to hit the bat with a tennis racket.	☐	☐	☐
(D) Sara and Ben hoped the bat would use echolocation to escape.	☐	☐	☐

1.   Raheem reads whenever he gets a chance. One of his all-time favorite books is *The Adventures of Roy Runner.* His older brother says that movies are never as good as the books they are based on. But when their family rented and watched *The Adventures of Roy Runner* together, Raheem thought it was fantastic. The actors and settings made the characters and scenes come alive even more. The few things that were added only enhanced the story.

2.   The cat watched the two people carefully. Although it was hungry and the food smelled good, the cat remained at a distance, watching. One of the two people began talking very loudly, whereupon the cat shrank farther back. A telephone rang, and the loud person got up to answer it. Meanwhile, the other person sat very still, with half-closed eyes. Nearby lay the remains of a partly eaten hamburger on a paper plate. Hungrily, the cat eyed the morsel. Then, ever so cautiously, the animal began to slink forward.

3.   Just as she had for the past few weekends, Gwen took a basketball to the playground at daybreak. Tryouts for the team were two weeks away, and she could get in a couple of hours of practice before anyone else wanted the court. In the cool, crisp dawn, she began practicing her shooting. She had not been at this long when her neighbor, Mel Daniels, a highly skilled basketball player, approached. "You're a good shot, Gwen," Mel remarked. "You haven't missed one, but you need more than shooting practice. You need some stiff competition too."

4.   Mr. and Mrs. Rollins strolled around the campus, visiting some of the places they had come to know over the past four years. "It's hard to believe we've been here only a few times a year," Mr. Rollins said.
     "It's harder to believe that four years have already gone by," answered Mrs. Rollins. "It seems like just yesterday that we brought Alicia here for the first time." The clock in the tower struck. Mr. and Mrs. Rollins joined a crowd of other people walking to the stadium where the ceremony would take place.

5.   Luisa had been putting her babysitting earnings into a special savings account for the past two years. Knowing this, her neighbors began calling her whenever any odd jobs needed doing. Mr. Anderson, who owned a local hardware store, even hired her to wait on customers before school. Practically every dollar that Luisa earned from these jobs went into her savings account. It wasn't easy for Luisa to completely give up buying pizzas, which she liked so much, but she felt strongly about going to college.

		T	F	I
1.	**(A)** Raheem's family rented the movie *The Adventures of Roy Runner*.	☐	☐	☐
	(B) Raheem's brother does not think books are as good as movies.	☐	☐	☐
	(C) Raheem does not think his brother's theory is always correct.	☐	☐	☐
	(D) Raheem likes to read.	☐	☐	☐

		T	F	I
2.	**(A)** The remains of the hamburger would not go to waste.	☐	☐	☐
	(B) No one got up to answer the telephone.	☐	☐	☐
	(C) The cat studied the two people.	☐	☐	☐
	(D) The cat was distrustful of loud-talking people.	☐	☐	☐

		T	F	I
3.	**(A)** Tryouts for the team were three weeks away.	☐	☐	☐
	(B) Mel and Gwen did not live near one another.	☐	☐	☐
	(C) Mel wanted to play basketball against Gwen.	☐	☐	☐
	(D) Mel complimented Gwen on her shooting ability.	☐	☐	☐

		T	F	I
4.	**(A)** This was the first time the Rollinses had been on campus.	☐	☐	☐
	(B) The ceremony would be held in the auditorium.	☐	☐	☐
	(C) Mr. and Mrs. Rollins were at their daughter Alicia's graduation.	☐	☐	☐
	(D) Crowds of people were going to the stadium.	☐	☐	☐

		T	F	I
5.	**(A)** Luisa was not especially fond of pizza.	☐	☐	☐
	(B) Luisa's neighbors hired her for odd jobs.	☐	☐	☐
	(C) Luisa made money from babysitting.	☐	☐	☐
	(D) Luisa's neighbors were pleased that she was saving money.	☐	☐	☐

1.   "Why would anyone be sawing so early?" Michael checked his alarm clock. "Eight in the morning," he mumbled. "People are trying to sleep, and that noisy chain saw's going. Somebody should complain."

    Michael looked at his alarm clock again. The numbers on it hadn't changed. He bolted out of bed. "What time is it?" he shouted.

    "It's two o'clock in the afternoon," answered his mother. "We were wondering if you were going to sleep all day."

    "Oh, no!" moaned Michael.

2.   The Phantoms' field hockey team excelled at offense. Their defense was another story. Because their goalie had moved away at the beginning of the season, the regular players had to take turns as goalie. The Phantoms would quickly rack up the goals, only to have their opponents do the same. The games were usually exciting and ended with high scores from both teams. Still the Phantoms wanted more wins.

3.   Have you ever wondered why popcorn pops? Have you ever noticed that some popcorn pops better than other popcorn? Regular corn kernels burn when they are exposed to heat. Popcorn actually comes from a certain type of corn. When the tightly sealed kernels of this corn are heated, tiny water droplets already inside the kernels convert to steam. Because the steam cannot escape through the tight seal, the kernel explodes.

4.   As Melanie pounded nails through the shutters, she saw dark clouds rushing in off the water. Blowing sand steadily blasted her legs.

    "Hurry up!" shouted Kate. "If we don't leave soon, the roads will be jammed with cars."

    "They gave us instructions only an hour ago," Melanie said. "We'll be fine. I want to put the patio furniture inside."

    As rain began to pelt the cottage roof, Kate bit her nails.

5.   "Have you seen the frilled lizard in the reptile habitat?" asked Kara.

    "It's pretty amazing," answered Josh.

    "It puffed up its frill and really surprised us," said Kara.

    "What is its frill?" asked Josh.

    "The frill is the large fan of skin on each side of its face that normally lies flat. It stands up when the lizard is frightened," she answered.

    "Wow, I'd like to see that," said Josh.

1. **(A)** A chain saw was making a loud noise.
   (B) Michael saw the numbers on his alarm clock change.
   (C) Michael's plans for the day were ruined because he had overslept.
   (D) Michael's mother said it was 2:00 P.M.

   T F I

2. **(A)** To win, the Phantoms need to improve their defense.
   (B) The Phantoms' goalie moved early in the season.
   (C) Opponents of the Phantoms rarely scored goals.
   (D) High scores in games did not mean wins for the Phantoms.

   T F I

3. **(A)** Any corn will pop if it has the right amount of moisture inside.
   (B) Some popcorn kernels pop better than others.
   (C) Popcorn that fails to pop may not have enough moisture inside.
   (D) Some types of corn kernels burn when they are heated.

   T F I

4. **(A)** Melanie wants to move the patio furniture to safety.
   (B) Kate is more nervous about the storm than Melanie.
   (C) Residents were told to evacuate because of an incoming storm.
   (D) The rain hasn't begun yet.

   T F I

5. **(A)** All lizards have a frill.
   (B) Josh saw the lizard but not the frill.
   (C) When Kara saw the frilled lizard, it must have been afraid.
   (D) The frilled lizard they saw lives in the reptile habitat.

   T F I

1.   "It's past your time to get up!" called Mrs. Halley. "Ethan, you'll be late for school if you don't hurry." Ethan heard his mom's voice through the thick covering of blankets. He was so tired he could hardly believe he had to get up. Last night he had gone to bed much later than usual. He had been studying feverishly for his math test and had lost track of time. "I'd better get up," Ethan said to himself, "or all that studying won't do me one bit of good."

2.   Maria had bought a new dress to wear to the dance. She had saved her allowance for three months to get enough money for the colorful outfit. "Try on your new dress," said her friend Samantha. "I want to see how it looks on you."
    Maria was more than happy to show off her new purchase. "Wait here," she answered as she skipped up the stairs. "I'll only be a minute." In no time at all, Maria was back, parading around the living room.

3.   Kimi stood alongside her teammates. She was next in line to bat. The game had not been going well; the opponents were leading by four runs. Kimi's team, the Vikings, had yet to score. Mrs. Barnes, the Vikings' coach, walked over to Kimi. "The most important thing for you to remember is to concentrate, Kimi," she said. "You have to keep your eye on the ball and think about nothing else but making contact." Kimi nodded and smiled weakly.

4.   Mrs. Guzman had never been in such a beautiful garden. The fragrance of roses filled the air. Everywhere she looked she could see the many-colored roses. "This is the most wonderful place in the world," she murmured to herself. "I would like to have a garden just like this." At that moment, Mrs. Guzman saw a gardener approach the new plantings. Without hesitation, Mrs. Guzman started toward him.

5.   Alison paced up and down the driveway. Uncle Fred was already ten minutes late. Last week they had made plans to go to the aquarium, where there was a special dolphin show that Alison had been looking forward to seeing. But if Uncle Fred didn't come soon, they would miss the show. Alison looked at her watch once again, grumbled something, and turned toward her bicycle.

Unit 11

		T	F	I

1. (A) Last night Ethan had gone to bed earlier than usual. ☐ ☐ ☐
   (B) Ethan would not be allowed to make up his test if he missed
   class the day of the test. ☐ ☐ ☐
   (C) The math test was scheduled for this day. ☐ ☐ ☐
   (D) It had been a cold night. ☐ ☐ ☐

---

2. (A) Samantha wanted Maria to put on the new dress. ☐ ☐ ☐
   (B) Maria did not want Samantha to see the new dress. ☐ ☐ ☐
   (C) It took Maria a long time to put on her new outfit. ☐ ☐ ☐
   (D) Maria was sure Samantha would like the dress. ☐ ☐ ☐

---

3. (A) Kimi had been having trouble concentrating. ☐ ☐ ☐
   (B) Kimi wasn't certain she could do the job. ☐ ☐ ☐
   (C) The Vikings were winning the game. ☐ ☐ ☐
   (D) Mrs. Barnes was the coach of Kimi's team. ☐ ☐ ☐

---

4. (A) Mrs. Guzman murmured a wish to herself. ☐ ☐ ☐
   (B) All the roses in the garden were shades of red. ☐ ☐ ☐
   (C) Mrs. Guzman was going to ask the gardener about starting
   a rose garden. ☐ ☐ ☐
   (D) The fragrance of roses filled the air. ☐ ☐ ☐

---

5. (A) Alison was going to ride off to the show alone. ☐ ☐ ☐
   (B) Alison and Uncle Fred had planned to attend a dolphin show. ☐ ☐ ☐
   (C) Alison wasn't looking forward to the show. ☐ ☐ ☐
   (D) The aquarium was within bike-riding distance of Alison's house. ☐ ☐ ☐

1. Grace Darling's dad kept Longstone Lighthouse on the Farne Islands off the northeast coast of England. On the night of September 6, 1838, the steamer *Forfarshire* was wrecked on the rocks. Nine men and women clung to the wreckage throughout the night.

    As soon as the morning light appeared, Grace and her dad rowed out through the still raging storm. They reached the wreck and brought the survivors back safely to the lighthouse.

2. The camp director told the two camp groups they could take either of two trails to the falls. The longer trail along the creek would be very wet, but the trail following the old logging road would be dry. The golden eagles arrived at the falls and stood around acting bored. The blue herons arrived later with muddy boots and talked excitedly about the muskrats, beaver, and water snake they saw.

3. Harriet Hosmer grew up in Watertown, Massachusetts, in the mid-1800s. She was independent and free-spirited from the time she was a child. When Harriet was 17, her father enrolled her in a boarding school in Lenox, Massachusetts. There Harriet met other young women, many of whom were interested in the arts. Harriet herself had a strong interest in sculpture. It was at this time that she made an important career decision.

4. Every year when Memorial Day approached, the Taylors, Samprases, and other families eagerly anticipated the Hallorans' yard sale. The Hallorans would carefully set out their collection of bicycles, skateboards, video games, and other items. The Hallorans needed to make room for their newly purchased acquisitions. Prices were reasonable, and the items were in nearly new condition. People in cars lined up early to survey the sale items.

5. Elizabeth Paterson, a beautiful young American woman from Baltimore, was just 16 when she married the 18-year-old Jerome Bonaparte, who afterward became a king in Europe. Jerome was the youngest brother of Emperor Napoleon Bonaparte.

    Years later the grandson of Jerome and Elizabeth, who served the United States as Secretary of the Navy and Attorney General, said, "He who serves his country well need not boast of an ancestry."

		T	F	I
1.	(A) Grace and her dad carried out their rescue mission in the darkness.	☐	☐	☐
	(B) Grace's dad was the keeper of Longstone Lighthouse.	☐	☐	☐
	(C) The Farne Islands are located off the coast of France.	☐	☐	☐
	(D) Grace was a courageous person.	☐	☐	☐

		T	F	I
2.	(A) The river trail had interesting wildlife to see.	☐	☐	☐
	(B) One of the camp groups saw blue herons.	☐	☐	☐
	(C) The two camp groups were named the blue herons and the golden eagles.	☐	☐	☐
	(D) The blue herons took the long, wet path along the creek.	☐	☐	☐

		T	F	I
3.	(A) Harriet Hosmer had been a timid child.	☐	☐	☐
	(B) She went to school in Lenox, Massachusetts.	☐	☐	☐
	(C) Harriet decided to pursue a career as a sculptor.	☐	☐	☐
	(D) Harriet had nothing in common with the other young women at the boarding school.	☐	☐	☐

		T	F	I
4.	(A) The Hallorans' annual yard sale takes place near Memorial Day.	☐	☐	☐
	(B) The Taylor and Sampras families like buying used items at good prices.	☐	☐	☐
	(C) The Hallorans like to shop at stores to buy new things.	☐	☐	☐
	(D) Skateboards, video games, and bicycles are among the sale items.	☐	☐	☐

		T	F	I
5.	(A) Jerome Bonaparte was an older brother of Napoleon Bonaparte.	☐	☐	☐
	(B) The grandson of Elizabeth and Jerome Bonaparte was not impressed with his royal ancestors.	☐	☐	☐
	(C) Jerome Bonaparte became a king.	☐	☐	☐
	(D) Elizabeth and Jerome Bonaparte were childless.	☐	☐	☐

October 15, 1948

Dear Maggie,

　　Boston is different than I expected. Sometimes I feel like I never left Dublin. All of our neighbors speak with Irish brogues. We can buy the same soda bread and tea that we buy at home, and it is almost as difficult to find work. Then when I walk into the North End of Boston, I feel like I'm in another country. I am viewed as an outsider but can purchase homemade strands of dough called pasta and see people enjoying a strong coffee drink called espresso. I can't understand a word they are saying because it's all in Italian . . .

A. Exercising Your Skill

The passage above could have been written by an Irish immigrant to a friend remaining in Ireland. People take risks or alter their course of action in the hope that it will create a better future for their families.

Throughout history, people have had *expectations,* or ideas, that a situation could be different or improved if they made a plan or acted in some way. For example, women working for suffrage believed that women deserved the right to vote.

With a group of students, come up with as many words or phrases as possible to describe the hopes and expectations people may have had during each time period below.

The time of:	
emancipation from slavery	settling of the American or Canadian West
California Gold Rush	early space exploration
creation of national parks	struggle for civil rights

B. Expanding Your Skill

Think about various details that might suggest different times in history. List each heading from the box above on a sheet of paper. Leave at least four line spaces below each heading. Then select words or phrases from the box below, and write them under the correct heading. Take the time to research words or phrases that you don't know. Under each heading add two more details that would fit.

Sputnik	Yellowstone	sodbusters
Martin Luther King Jr.	Emancipation Proclamation	Frederick Douglass
buffalo slaughter	Cochise	prairie schooners
segregation	abolitionists	"whites only"
Susan B. Anthony	John Glenn	satellites
conservation	bus boycott	Sutter's Mill
stake a claim	19th Amendment	endangered landscapes

C. Exploring Language

Choose one of the time periods from Part A. Do additional research to learn more about it. Write two journal entries as if you were a person living during that time. Be sure to add colorful details that provide information about that time. Use detailed language to describe your character's feelings.

After you are finished, share your entries with a partner. From the information you included, your partner should be able to answer some of the following questions.

- What did the people of the time wear and eat?

- What were their major problems or concerns?

- What was unique about the time?

- What was a typical day like for your character?

- In general, how was life easier or more difficult than today?

D. Expressing Yourself

Choose one of these activities.

1. Find the comics section in a newspaper. Study one comic strip to understand what motivates its characters to think and act the way they do. Then choose a period in history on which to base your own comic strip. Think about a problem or issue your characters face in their time period, and show how they work to solve the problem. As you draw, be sure to include plenty of historical details such as clothing and surroundings.

2. Imagine that you and a partner are friends living during the same time in history and that you write letters to each other from different locations. For example, one friend might live in the city while the other lives on the frontier. First make a list of details unique to your time and place. Include food, clothing, equipment or tools, expectations, and concerns. Then write your letters. Read your letters aloud to the rest of the class. If you have time, write a reply to your partner's letter.

1.   Windows sometimes allow us to see our reflections, but mirrors always show reflections. This is because the backs of mirrors are coated with a special silver coating that stops light from passing through. Both mirrors and windows are made from shiny glass. Light that hits glass bounces back when what is on the other side is dark or opaque. The reflecting light shows the subject's reflection.

2.   Rafael stared at the X-ray machine. He had seen one once at the dentist's office, but he never thought that one would be used on Sam. Sam was wrapped in a blanket and resting quietly in Rafael's lap. The veterinarian had given the collie a shot and told Rafael that his dog was not in pain. "The X-ray is just to make sure that all is well," he said. "Sam will probably be running again in a week or so, but you must keep him from chasing cars."

3.   Monica looks closely at Howard Ross for a few minutes. At first Howard sits rather stiffly, but then he starts to relax a bit. *Now,* thinks Monica, *he looks more natural.* Monica looks at his face until she understands its shape. She studies the way the light plays on his skin, making patterns of lights and shadows. She studies the color of his hair, his eyes, and his skin. Only then does she turn to pick up a brush and dip it into the oil paints.

4.   Alexis stared at the unfinished science report. It was due tomorrow, and there were hours of work to do on it. *I don't mind working,* Alexis thought, *but the game is tomorrow.* She picked up the phone to call her soccer coach. She could imagine what he would say: "You know the rule. It's up to you." Alexis knew the rule. Missing practice meant not playing the next game. But it was her fault that the report hadn't been completed. She straightened her back as she heard the coach answer the phone.

5.   Hannah kept one spare house key hidden under a rock in the garden. Then if the keys in her purse were ever lost, she'd be able to get back into her own house. Coming home late one night, Hannah realized that she'd forgotten to put the keys back in her purse. She had left her keys at work! Sighing with weariness, she got her spare house key from under the rock, let herself into the house, and fell into bed. Several days later, Hannah misplaced her purse. When she returned home and looked under the rock for her spare key, it wasn't there.

		T	**F**	**I**
1.	**(A)** Mirrors always show reflections.	☐	☐	☐
	(B) Mirrors are made from old windows.	☐	☐	☐
	(C) Windows with darkness on one side may show reflections.	☐	☐	☐
	(D) Light passing through transparent glass does not reflect well.	☐	☐	☐

		T	**F**	**I**
2.	**(A)** The dog was suffering pain.	☐	☐	☐
	(B) Rafael had never seen an X-ray machine before.	☐	☐	☐
	(C) Rafael's dog, Sam, had been hit by a car.	☐	☐	☐
	(D) Sam was wrapped in a blanket.	☐	☐	☐

		T	**F**	**I**
3.	**(A)** Howard Ross grows tenser the longer he sits.	☐	☐	☐
	(B) Monica observes her subject very carefully.	☐	☐	☐
	(C) Monica uses pastel chalk for her work.	☐	☐	☐
	(D) Monica will paint Howard's portrait.	☐	☐	☐

		T	**F**	**I**
4.	**(A)** Alexis was working on a science report.	☐	☐	☐
	(B) Alexis was aware of the rule about missing practice.	☐	☐	☐
	(C) Alexis decided to miss practice to finish the report.	☐	☐	☐
	(D) Alexis heard the coach's wife answer the phone.	☐	☐	☐

		T	**F**	**I**
5.	**(A)** Hannah kept her only spare house key hidden under the doormat.	☐	☐	☐
	(B) When Hannah had left her keys at work, she found the house key under the rock.	☐	☐	☐
	(C) After Hannah misplaced her purse, she found the house key under the rock.	☐	☐	☐
	(D) Hannah had forgotten to put her house key back underneath the rock.	☐	☐	☐

1.   Drew trudged down the street, his bat thrown over his shoulder and his cap pulled down over his eyes. Dirt stains covered every inch of his uniform. He looked straight ahead, ignoring his friends who waved to him from the park. As he approached the house, his mom looked out the kitchen window. Just then Drew lifted the bat over his shoulder and slammed it into the ground. Mrs. Nelson was not happy with her son's action.

2.   Jasmine felt nervous as, from her position backstage, she watched her classmates perform. She had expected to be a little scared, but she had not thought she would feel such a mass of butterflies in her stomach. Mr. Kanu had given the whole class a lecture about opening-night jitters. He explained that people always feel nervous the first time they perform in front of an audience. *Wow! Was he right!* thought Jasmine. *I think I'll practice my lines one more time.*

3.   Sam knew how easy it was to let homework slide. He had a habit of waiting until just before bedtime to start his work. This meant he was often too tired to concentrate on his assignments. *Maybe my teacher can help me organize my after-school time the way he encouraged my friend, Luanda, to work out a schedule,* thought Sam. *If I do my homework immediately after school, maybe I'll do a better job.* Sam decided to tell Mr. Tsumori his idea. Sam was sure Mr. Tsumori would have more good suggestions for getting the homework done.

4.   Matthew, now in his senior year, had studied very hard for the final math test. He had decided to work as hard as he could all month in order to get an A in math on his report card. Matthew's dad had helped him study. He had explained some formulas that Matthew did not understand and had also made up extra problems for Matthew to work on. *The extra work really paid off,* thought Matthew. *I knew how to solve all the questions on the test. I probably didn't make any mistakes at all.*

5.   "What's wrong with you?" asked Logan. "You look sad."
       "I *am* sad," replied Teddy forlornly. "Mom won't let me start a yard-cleaning service. My friend Owen and I had a great idea for making money. We were going to put an advertisement in the paper telling people about our new service. Then they would hire us to take care of their yards."
       "Omar Rashid has that kind of business," said Logan, "but he's much older than you."

Unit 14

1. **(A)** Drew's friends waved to him.
   (B) Drew was upset over the baseball game he had just played.
   (C) Mrs. Nelson was not happy to see Drew throw down his bat.
   (D) Drew's uniform was spotless.

   T F I

2. **(A)** Jasmine was worried that her nervousness would cause her to forget her part.
   (B) Mr. Kanu knows that stage fright is to be expected.
   (C) Jasmine was the first performer to go onstage.
   (D) Jasmine disagreed with what Mr. Kanu had said about opening-night jitters.

   T F I

3. **(A)** Mr. Tsumori has a reputation for helping his students.
   (B) Luanda was Sam's friend.
   (C) Sam was often too tired to give full attention to his studies.
   (D) Luanda had gotten no help from Mr. Tsumori.

   T F I

4. **(A)** Matthew had done a lot of extra studying in math.
   (B) Matthew was in his senior year.
   (C) Matthew is going to get his A in math.
   (D) Matthew's dad couldn't understand the formulas.

   T F I

5. **(A)** Teddy's mom wanted Owen and Teddy to start a yard-cleaning business.
   (B) Teddy and Owen wanted to put an ad in the paper.
   (C) Omar Rashid has a yard-cleaning business.
   (D) Logan thought that Teddy and Owen were too young to start a yard-cleaning service.

   T F I

Unit 15

1. Amos had paused at the front door for a few seconds, as if hoping to gain entrance. His shiny black hair glistened in the sun. His wide-open green eyes gazed around expectantly. Then he turned and began walking very slowly away from the house. He stopped for a moment to stretch his legs and back.

"Are you hungry?" asked the boy in the house, opening the door. "Come on, I'll give you something to eat."

Without sounding a reply, Amos bounded into the house and headed straight for the kitchen. A fish dinner and some warm milk awaited him.

2. Sarah broke the surface of the water with a gasp. She spotted the judges on the shore and began stroking steadily toward them. As she raised her head to inhale, she caught glimpses of Nell and Olivia. Nell was several yards behind her, but Olivia was even with her. *Should I make the push now,* thought Sarah, *or wait until the last ten yards?* Sarah remembered that Olivia often lost strength during the last quarter of a race—which was right about now. *Here I go!* exclaimed Sarah.

3. "What will you get Mom for her birthday?" Chris asked Monica.

"I've been thinking about getting her some new gardening tools," said Monica. "The ones she has are all bent and rusty."

"Well, if we went in together on a present," suggested Chris, "we could get her what she really wants and needs."

"What's that?" asked Monica.

"A riding lawn mower!" replied Chris. "You know how she works pushing that old hand mower around the yard."

"Great idea!" agreed Monica.

4. "I wonder why they're building that skyscraper backwards?" said Mr. Heath. "It doesn't seem logical to complete it from the top down."

"I read a brief news article about that new building method," said Mrs. Drew. "First they build the frame. Then they hang the outer skin of the building on the frame from the top down. The outside of the building comes in sections. Each section has hooks that let it hang on the frame."

"That's very interesting," said Mr. Heath. "Do they always begin hanging the sections from the top, or could they start anywhere?"

"I've no idea," said Mrs. Drew. "I've told all I know about it."

5. Kendra's dad hammered in the last stake and looked doubtfully at the tent. "I see we have another small tear in the side. I'd better fix it right now. No telling if we might have a little rain tonight."

"Will the tent be all right, Dad?" asked Kendra.

"Oh, sure, but we'll retire 'old faithful' here after this camping trip and get a new one for next summer."

1. **(A)** Amos is a cat.   T F I
   (B) The boy gave Amos a fish dinner and some warm milk.
   (C) Amos turned and walked away from the house after the boy called him.
   (D) Amos had eaten at the boy's house before.

2. **(A)** Sarah had a good chance of winning the race.   T F I
   (B) Sarah was several yards ahead of Nell.
   (C) Olivia always sped up during the last quarter.
   (D) Sarah didn't think Nell would win the race.

3. **(A)** Monica had been thinking about getting her mom some gardening tools.   T F I
   (B) Chris wanted to get the old hand mower sharpened.
   (C) Mom's present gardening tools are rusty.
   (D) Mom prefers useful presents to impractical gifts.

4. **(A)** Mrs. Drew told Mr. Heath what she knew about the building method.   T F I
   (B) The news article hadn't given full details of the new method.
   (C) Mr. Heath wondered why the builders were constructing the skyscraper backwards.
   (D) Mr. Heath wasn't interested in the building method.

5. **(A)** Kendra wondered if the tent would be all right.   T F I
   (B) The tent had a small tear in the side.
   (C) The family had been camping often before.
   (D) Kendra's dad referred to the tent as "old ironsides."

1. Jill bounced her tennis racket against her palm in despair. "It's easy to see that I'm not a tennis pro," she said. "As hard as I work on my serve, I can't seem to get it right. Even my best friends are telling me I should try another sport."

    "It's your choice," said the coach. "Do you want to follow your friends' advice?"

    Jill adjusted her headband and said, "I'll try again."

2. The two grown sisters strolled together, each lost in her own thoughts. "Yes, I remember," Vicki said quietly. "Every morning I'd feed the chickens and gather the eggs. Dad would milk the cows, and you," she laughed fondly, "you were usually still asleep."

    "I always was a late sleeper, wasn't I?" Joan replied. "It's a good thing you were an early riser, Vicki, or the chores may never have been done." They both laughed again and then walked on.

3. "The washing machine broke down this morning, and I had to call for a repairperson again," said John's mom.

    "Will it be the same repairperson who came last time?" asked John.

    "I hope not," his mom answered. "He wasn't any better than the person before him. In fact, neither of them seemed to know what to do. I asked for someone different. The company is sending an expert, so they say. They realize that a machine that has broken down several times doesn't set a very good record, especially for a machine that is only two months old!"

4. "I'm not used to this kind of exercise," said Mr. Fong as he puffed up another flight of stairs.

    "Who is?" Mrs. Clay asked. "But you are luckier than I am. You work on the sixth floor. I have to go up to the tenth. And I really feel sorry for people going to offices on the 20th floor."

    "Well, I guess I am lucky," Mr. Fong replied. "But I still hope the mechanic gets here soon."

    "Just think of all the weight we're losing," said Mrs. Clay.

5. "Did you finish all the algebra homework?" Jake asked his friends.

    "I did everything except the last three problems. I just couldn't figure them out," answered Kiri.

    "I had trouble with those too," said Vito. "I thought maybe Mitsu could explain them to me."

    "I was going to ask Mitsu about them too," Jake commented.

    "That's a good idea," Kiri said. "Let's see if we can talk with Mitsu before class starts."

		T	F	I

1. **(A)** The coach told Jill it was her choice whether or not to follow her friends' advice. ☐ ☐ ☐
   (B) Jill said she couldn't get her serve right. ☐ ☐ ☐
   (C) Jill wants to be a good tennis player. ☐ ☐ ☐
   (D) Jill believes she plays tennis like a professional. ☐ ☐ ☐

2. **(A)** Joan had never been an early riser. ☐ ☐ ☐
   (B) Vicki had usually fed the chickens and gathered the eggs. ☐ ☐ ☐
   (C) The sisters had spent their childhood on a farm. ☐ ☐ ☐
   (D) Joan had milked the cows every morning. ☐ ☐ ☐

3. **(A)** The washing machine has never broken before. ☐ ☐ ☐
   (B) Mom had asked for a different repairperson. ☐ ☐ ☐
   (C) Neither John nor his mom knows how to fix the washing machine. ☐ ☐ ☐
   (D) Mom said the man who tried to fix the machine last time was better than the repairperson before him. ☐ ☐ ☐

4. **(A)** The elevator in the building where Mr. Fong and Mrs. Clay work is broken. ☐ ☐ ☐
   (B) Mr. Fong works on the tenth floor. ☐ ☐ ☐
   (C) Mrs. Clay said to think about the pounds they were losing. ☐ ☐ ☐
   (D) Mr. Fong puffed as he went up the stairs. ☐ ☐ ☐

5. **(A)** Jake, Kiri, and Vito want to ask Mitsu for explanations. ☐ ☐ ☐
   (B) Mitsu is a good algebra student. ☐ ☐ ☐
   (C) Kiri finished all the algebra homework. ☐ ☐ ☐
   (D) Vito had trouble with the last three problems. ☐ ☐ ☐

1.   Esperanza thought her speech went well. Afterward people she didn't even know from each of the three grades said they would vote for her. Conner's speech was funny, but his delivery suggested that he didn't take the job very seriously. His popularity would definitely help him in his bid for the leadership position. Whenever she saw Conner in the hallway, students were giving him the high five.

2.   "I don't know," said Amy. "I've never tried the long jump."

"Go ahead!" said Dan. "All that can happen is that you won't jump very far. At the worst you might trip and fall, the way Harry did."

"And that would be embarrassing with everyone watching," replied Amy.

"Embarrassing!" Dan laughed. "Why are you so worried about what everyone else thinks? Harry didn't care."

3.   Joe's brow wrinkled. "I don't understand," he said. "This coupon from the newspaper offers a free sandwich and soda to anyone at this fast-food restaurant all this week. The place should be busy, but hardly anyone is here."

"Did you read the small print on the coupon?" asked Marta. "I've learned to do that. It says, 'This offer good at participating restaurants only.'"

4.   For her science fair project, Dana had to investigate an issue or process related to everyday life at home. She had often seen her dad drop a penny into the water after picking a bouquet of flowers from their garden. She also heard that a small amount of bleach or store-purchased preservative could be used for keeping flowers fresh. She wondered which of the three methods would work best.

5.   Manuel had been doing odd jobs for three months to get enough money to buy the video game "Space Paraders." "I finally have enough money!" exclaimed Manuel one Saturday afternoon as he counted the bills he had saved.

Manuel headed straight for the video store. As he approached, he saw in the window a sign reading, "Today Only! Thirty percent off the video games listed below!"

"All right!" cheered Manuel as he bounded through the door.

	T	F	I
1. **(A)** Conner's speech was humorous.	☐	☐	☐
(B) Conner and Esperanza are running for school president.	☐	☐	☐
(C) More people know Esperanza than Conner.	☐	☐	☐
(D) Esperanza's speech was more serious than Conner's.	☐	☐	☐

	T	F	I
2. **(A)** Dan said Amy might trip and fall.	☐	☐	☐
(B) Amy didn't like the thought of failure.	☐	☐	☐
(C) Harry appeared to be embarrassed when he fell.	☐	☐	☐
(D) Amy had never tried the long jump.	☐	☐	☐

	T	F	I
3. **(A)** This fast-food restaurant was not participating in the offer.	☐	☐	☐
(B) The coupon offered two free items.	☐	☐	☐
(C) Marta had been fooled by coupons before.	☐	☐	☐
(D) Joe asked Marta if she had read the small print.	☐	☐	☐

	T	F	I
4. **(A)** Dana had a science fair project to complete.	☐	☐	☐
(B) Dana's science fair project had to do with a question about her everyday life.	☐	☐	☐
(C) Dana might compare the effectiveness of bleach, preservative, and a copper penny for keeping flowers fresh.	☐	☐	☐
(D) The flowers under investigation would be potted in soil.	☐	☐	☐

	T	F	I
5. **(A)** The video game "Space Paraders" was on sale that day.	☐	☐	☐
(B) Manuel had saved enough money for the game.	☐	☐	☐
(C) Manuel had borrowed money to buy "Space Paraders."	☐	☐	☐
(D) Manuel saw the sign about the game sale in the window.	☐	☐	☐

1.   "Dad called to say that he'll be late getting home from work," said Emma. "We'll have to make our own supper."

"Well, that shouldn't be too difficult," responded Kate. "There are hamburger patties, frozen dinners, and many other foods in the freezer. We can cook something in the microwave oven. I'll have a hamburger."

"I don't feel like eating a hamburger," replied Emma. "May I take another look?"

"Go ahead," said Kate. "But don't take too long to make up your mind. I've made up mine."

---

2.   John stood on his seat at the baseball stadium. "It looks as if our team will lose," he declared. "It's the bottom half of the ninth inning, we're behind by two runs, and we have only one more chance at bat."

"You may be right," replied Elisa. "But we have two people on base with our cleanup hitter coming up to bat."

Then the crowd in the stands cheered as the batter dug in and connected with a fastball. Soon, however, the people groaned as they saw the opposing team's left fielder moving easily toward the ball.

---

3.   The space shuttle stood ready on its launching pad. "If the weather remains clear," stated the mission controller, "we'll begin liftoff in exactly three hours."

For the next hour the sky remained clear. Then, as the second hour approached, clouds darkened the sky until it seemed that launching the shuttle would be impossible. Finally, as the third hour drew near, bright sunlight peeked through the clouds.

---

4.   "I wish I knew why my car won't run now," grumbled Mrs. Johnson. "The mechanic said he had repaired the problem."

Lucy peered under the hood. "Did he tell you what he fixed?" questioned her daughter.

"Yes," answered Mrs. Johnson. "He said he installed a new distributor cap and new spark plugs."

Lucy smiled. "That's good," she commented. "But did you ask him whether he checked the fuel filter and the battery?"

Mrs. Johnson looked at her daughter in bewilderment.

---

5.   Only two miles remained. Tony was just behind the second-place bicyclist when his wheel accidentally caught that of the other racer's, sending his competitor down in a nasty crash. It looked like Tony's chance to pull up next to the lead. Then he thought about the fallen rider. Tony's sense of sportsmanship won out, and he began to dismount. Later when he crossed the finish line, the crowd cheered appreciatively.

		T	F	I
1.	**(A)** Kate said they could cook something in the microwave oven.	☐	☐	☐
	(B) Emma and Kate will not eat the same thing for supper.	☐	☐	☐
	(C) Emma said she felt like eating a hamburger.	☐	☐	☐
	(D) There were other foods in the freezer besides hamburger patties and frozen dinners.	☐	☐	☐

		T	F	I
2.	**(A)** The cleanup hitter swung at and missed the fastball.	☐	☐	☐
	(B) The left fielder caught the ball that the batter hit.	☐	☐	☐
	(C) John and Elisa's team lost the game.	☐	☐	☐
	(D) It was the bottom half of the ninth inning.	☐	☐	☐

		T	F	I
3.	**(A)** The mission controller said that liftoff would take place "rain or shine."	☐	☐	☐
	(B) The mission controller said that the liftoff could begin in exactly three hours.	☐	☐	☐
	(C) For three hours after the controller's statement, the sky remained perfectly clear.	☐	☐	☐
	(D) The space shuttle would be launched according to the original schedule.	☐	☐	☐

		T	F	I
4.	**(A)** Mrs. Johnson had not asked about the fuel filter and the battery.	☐	☐	☐
	(B) The mechanic had installed a new alternator and water pump.	☐	☐	☐
	(C) Lucy knew more about car motors than her mother.	☐	☐	☐
	(D) Mrs. Johnson wondered why her car wouldn't run after it had been repaired.	☐	☐	☐

		T	F	I
5.	**(A)** Tony was in a close bicycle race.	☐	☐	☐
	(B) Tony won the race.	☐	☐	☐
	(C) The crowd cheered Tony for his good sportsmanship.	☐	☐	☐
	(D) Tony was in third place when the crash happened.	☐	☐	☐

1. Blake's classes at his new school were on two different floors and sometimes at opposite ends of the building. He had only three minutes to walk through the crowded hallways to get to his classes. His health teacher had given him three late notices, and he earned another in math. Fortunately, he recently found a shortcut down a set of stairs and a hallway used by only a few students.

2. Located in the heart of New Jersey is a wilderness of one thousand square miles of pine forests and swamps known as the Pine Barrens. This area lies roughly between the cities of Asbury Park and Cape May. Mile after mile of stunted pine trees—some only three feet tall—grow in the sandy soil of the region. While the farming of conventional crops is not profitable, cranberries and blueberries grow well in the poor soil of the Pine Barrens.

3. Have you noticed how much cooler it is if you sit under a tree? Trees provide welcome shade from the hot sun and keep homes cooler, but shade is not the only reason it's cool under trees. If conditions are right, tree leaves actually cool the surrounding air. Leaves can release moisture that causes a cooling effect as it evaporates. It is almost as if trees act as nature's air conditioners.

4. Someday soon, people may be traveling to Mars! Scientists, astronauts, and politicians are planning such a journey, possibly to be shared by the United States and Russia. Scientists plan to build an orbiting space station from which the mission would take off. The trip just to get to Mars would take two to three years, because Mars is 35 million miles from Earth—160 times the distance to the moon. People who will be selected for the flight have already been dubbed "Marsnauts."

5. "I want a gold watch, a sports car, and a boat," said Lee.
   "Will that be it?" asked his mom. "Are you by any chance like the man who owned the goose with the golden eggs?"
   "I've forgotten that silly old story," said Lee.
   "Well," continued his mom, "the man wasn't satisfied with just the one golden egg that the goose laid each day, so he killed and cut open the goose, looking for more."
   "What did he find?" asked Lee, suddenly interested.
   "He found that the goose, inside, wasn't any different from any other goose," replied his mom.

1. **(A)** Blake's classes were all on the third floor. T F I
(B) Blake was new to the school.
(C) Health class was Blake's most challenging to get to on time.
(D) Blake believed his new route would save him time traveling to classes.

---

2. **(A)** New Jersey's wilderness was named the Pine Barrens because its poor soil can produce only stunted pine trees. T F I
(B) The Pine Barrens extends from Cape May to Asbury Park.
(C) Giant pine trees grow in the dense forests of the Pine Barrens.
(D) Blueberries and cranberries grow well in the sandy soil of New Jersey's wilderness.

---

3. **(A)** Trees keeps people even cooler than they might realize. T F I
(B) Many people plant trees to replace their air conditioners.
(C) Trees give shelter from the sun.
(D) Homes sheltered by trees could have lower summer energy costs.

---

4. **(A)** People from Russia and the U.S. might share the trip to Mars. T F I
(B) The journey to Mars would take two to three years.
(C) "Marsnauts" will be people selected by NASA.
(D) Mars is the same distance from Earth as the moon is.

---

5. **(A)** Lee had remembered word for word the story "The Goose with the Golden Eggs." T F I
(B) Before the man killed the goose, the bird had laid a golden egg daily.
(C) Lee's mom felt that he was getting greedy.
(D) The man discovered that the inside of the goose was the same as the inside of any other goose.

"Did you finish all the algebra homework?" Jake asked his friends.

"I did everything except the last three problems. I just couldn't figure them out," answered Kiri.

"I had trouble with those too," said Vito. "I thought maybe Mitsu could explain them to me."

"That's a good idea," Kiri said. "Let's see if we can talk with Mitsu before class starts."

A. Exercising Your Skill

Although the passage above does not come right out and say it, you can guess that Mitsu likes algebra and is quite good at this subject. Stories often give strong clues about the characters' qualities and wishes without stating them directly. Look at the sample item below. You can figure out that "Someone who watches a lot of television probably *knows the names of several popular television shows.*" Now read the sentence starters and think about the clues that are given. Figure out what someone with these qualities or wishes probably would do, think, or feel. Write each sentence starter on your paper, and complete it with your own ending. When you are finished, compare your sentences with your classmates' sentences.

Example: Someone who watches a lot of television probably <u>knows the names of several popular television shows</u>.

1. Someone who wants to do well on a science test probably _____.

2. Someone who is a good artist probably _____.

3. Someone who likes a particular author probably _____.

4. Someone who wants to become a carpenter probably _____.

5. Someone whose dog recently died probably _____.

6. Someone who loves bright colors probably _____.

B. Expanding Your Skill

Choose a partner and play a "Chances Are" game. Take turns beginning and completing statements like the two below. Be sure that your statements give clues about a person or character so that your partner can tell what he or she does or is like.

Paul hardly puffs after running up the hill.

Chances are <u>Paul exercises regularly</u>.

Miss Tipton can easily tell a flower from a weed.

Chances are <u>Miss Tipton is an experienced gardener</u>.

C. Exploring Language

Read the two paragraph starters below. Choose one of them, and expand the idea into a complete paragraph, adding three or four more sentences. Include information in your paragraph that will most likely show the goals or qualities of the character based on the original statements.

1. Dr. Ruiz, a dedicated archaeologist, had been tirelessly searching for the ruins in the steamy jungle for almost two weeks. Now the guides were warning her of possible danger ahead.

2. Ken was a strong but safety-conscious swimmer. Slicing through the waves with his powerful strokes, Ken suddenly realized he had swum out much farther than usual.

Opening Sentence _____

Detail 1: _____

Detail 2: _____

Detail 3: _____

Closing Sentence: _____

D. Expressing Yourself

Choose one of these activities.

1. Exchange paragraphs from Part C with a classmate. Add one or two more details about the character based on what has been written so far in the paragraph. Ask your partner if he or she agrees with your ideas.

2. From an old magazine cut out a picture of someone doing an activity, such as jogging, eating, teaching children, playing a sport, or operating a tractor. Make up a short story about the person in the picture. Include information about the person's likes and dislikes based on details in the picture. Share your pictures and stories with your classmates. Ask them whether your story about the picture makes sense and why.

3. Create a colorful picture of yourself doing what you enjoy most. Show your picture to your classmates and see if they can guess what your favorite activity is.

1.   Marina often went with her mom to do her mystery shopping. For her job, Marina's mom had to fill out different questionnaires, answering questions about the service provided. Sometimes an assignment took them to a restaurant. The staff at the stores and restaurants was completely unaware that she and her mom were not regular customers. Usually the person who waited on them received a good report, but occasionally the report was negative.

2.   Samantha and her brother Nick had been indoors for the last three days. A winter storm was preventing them from going to high school and was keeping them inside the apartment. The strong winds, combined with subzero temperatures, had made venturing outside unthinkable. Snow and freezing rain had transformed the city streets into a treacherous icescape. When the sun finally broke through, a world of sparkling crystal formations appeared. Samantha nearly ran her brother down in her rush to get to the elevator. The elevator signal pointed to "Down."

3.   Carla had begun playing tennis when she was eight years old. Her early life had been a succession of vigorous lessons, exhausting matches, and a series of ever-more-important tournaments. More often than not, Carla had emerged victorious. She proved she had the talent and determination to become a true champion. Now those endless hours of practice and matches were about to pay off. The moment Carla had dreamed of and worked so hard for had finally arrived.

4.   Jake was excited to visit New York. He had heard all his life about the Statue of Liberty. He was fascinated by bridges, and he planned to visit the Brooklyn Bridge. "Rahway," "Elizabeth," "Newark," said the conductor as each stop brought him closer. His heart pounded. Soon he would be at Penn Station. Would he be able to find the correct subway line to travel up to his uncle's neighborhood?

5.   "And here is where we receive current forecasts from the National Weather Service," the weather forecaster explained to Kim and her classmates. "We get information on temperature, moisture, barometric pressure, and wind speed and direction," he continued.

      "Does the service provide any other information?" asked Kim.

      "Yes, it gives special information to people in aviation and marine industries, to forest rangers, and to farmers. It also provides us with important storm information," he concluded.

	T	F	I
1. (A) Marina's mom was looking for a job.	☐	☐	☐
(B) Marina's mom is paid to report on the quality of service.	☐	☐	☐
(C) Workers treat Marina and her mom like regular customers.	☐	☐	☐
(D) The service Marina and her mom received was usually good.	☐	☐	☐

	T	F	I
2. (A) Samantha and Nick were in high school.	☐	☐	☐
(B) After three days of stormy weather, the sun came out.	☐	☐	☐
(C) Illness had prevented Nick and Samantha from attending school.	☐	☐	☐
(D) Samantha was tired of having to stay indoors.	☐	☐	☐

	T	F	I
3. (A) Carla had developed her talent through practice.	☐	☐	☐
(B) Carla had begun playing tennis as soon as she could walk.	☐	☐	☐
(C) Carla didn't care about being a champion tennis player.	☐	☐	☐
(D) Carla was about to play in the most important tournament of her career.	☐	☐	☐

	T	F	I
4. (A) This was Jake's first trip to New York City.	☐	☐	☐
(B) The Statue of Liberty was one of the stops mentioned by the conductor.	☐	☐	☐
(C) Jake's mode of transportation was train.	☐	☐	☐
(D) Jake was somewhat nervous as he approached the city.	☐	☐	☐

	T	F	I
5. (A) National Weather Service gives information on temperature and wind speed.	☐	☐	☐
(B) The service also provides important storm information.	☐	☐	☐
(C) The service is used by forecasters only.	☐	☐	☐
(D) Service information helps forecasters predict storms.	☐	☐	☐

1. Jacob's dog, Wolf, was missing. Jacob cried and cried.

    "Don't cry," said Jacob's parents. "We'll get you a new dog."

    "Maybe we'll find a dog similar to Wolf," said Jacob's mother.

    Jacob and his mother looked at the dogs in an animal shelter. Jacob saw one dog that looked familiar. He looked again. It was Wolf! Someone had found Wolf and turned the dog over to the shelter.

2. Melanie couldn't figure out what happened. She had carefully saved her document in its folder before closing, but when she looked in the folder the next day, nothing was there. Other odd things were happening. Friends told her to be on the lookout for the devastating "hello there" virus. She had carelessly downloaded images and opened plenty of unusual e-mail messages lately. Could she be a victim?

3. Ryahd purchased one ticket after another. He couldn't believe it was that difficult to throw a softball into a basket. Yet toss after toss ended up bouncing out. He finally gave up when he couldn't buy any more tickets. Then when his friend Daniel wanted him to ride with him on the Zip the Loop, Ryahd ended up having to stand and watch. At next year's fair he planned to have a different strategy.

4. "Hey, look at this strange shell!" called out Ines. She bent down and picked up a smooth green disk. Aunt Carol ran over to her.

    "That's very pretty," said Aunt Carol, "but it's not a shell. It looks like a shell, but I think it's part of a bottle."

    "A bottle!" said Ines. "What are you talking about? It doesn't look anything like a bottle to me. Why do you think that?"

    "Because it's glass," said Aunt Carol. "There's lettering on the other side that says 'Bottled in New Jersey.' Let's put that in the trash."

5. Josh wanted the bicycle he had seen, but it cost 150 dollars. He wondered where he'd get that much money.

    "There's only one way you're going to be able to pay for that bicycle," said his mom. "Put away part of your allowance every week."

    Each week Josh put money into the bank on his dresser. Months passed. *I wonder if I've saved enough for the bike,* Josh said to himself. He opened his bank and counted his savings. "Three hundred dollars," breathed Josh. "With this much money I could buy two bicycles!"

1. **(A)** Wolf was a terrier.
   (B) Jacob found his missing dog at an animal shelter.
   (C) Wolf had had no identification tag when the person found her.
   (D) Jacob's parents did not want to get him another dog.

   T F I
   ☐ ☐ ☐
   ☐ ☐ ☐
   ☐ ☐ ☐
   ☐ ☐ ☐

2. **(A)** Melanie's document was missing from its folder.
   (B) Melanie was worried that her computer had a virus.
   (C) Friends sent Melanie viruses on purpose.
   (D) Melanie's recent computer activities led to the problems.

   T F I
   ☐ ☐ ☐
   ☐ ☐ ☐
   ☐ ☐ ☐
   ☐ ☐ ☐

3. **(A)** Daniel had talked Ryahd into spending all his money on a game.
   (B) The Zip the Loop was a ride at the fair.
   (C) Ryahd was happy he chose to play the game over and over.
   (D) The softball game looked much easier than it was.

   T F I
   ☐ ☐ ☐
   ☐ ☐ ☐
   ☐ ☐ ☐
   ☐ ☐ ☐

4. **(A)** The lettering on the glass said "Bottled in Boston."
   (B) The disk Ines found was covered with bumps.
   (C) Aunt Carol commented on how pretty Ines's "find" was.
   (D) Aunt Carol was afraid the glass's sharp edge would hurt Ines.

   T F I
   ☐ ☐ ☐
   ☐ ☐ ☐
   ☐ ☐ ☐
   ☐ ☐ ☐

5. **(A)** Josh kept his bank on the dresser.
   (B) Josh had not kept track of the money he had put into the bank.
   (C) The bicycle Josh wanted cost 150 dollars.
   (D) Josh's mom told him to put his entire allowance away each week.

   T F I
   ☐ ☐ ☐
   ☐ ☐ ☐
   ☐ ☐ ☐
   ☐ ☐ ☐

1. "What do you think about the announcement the president made last night?" Joe asked his friend Michael.

"What announcement?" Michael asked. "I haven't heard anything about it."

Joe was surprised. "Are you serious? It was the main news in the papers and on the radio this morning."

"Oh, really? It must be quite important," Michael said. "I'll bet you had a chance to hear the final score of the hockey game on the news too. How did it turn out?"

---

2. "I'm going to sign up for the CPR class today," Olivia told Madison.

"What's CPR?" Madison wanted to know.

"Cardiopulmonary resuscitation," said Olivia. "It's emergency treatment for someone who can't breathe. A person having a heart attack needs it. Don't you remember when Mrs. Castillo's father had a heart attack, and she saved his life because she knew how to do CPR? I've been wanting to learn ever since."

---

3. "As you all know," stated Coach Hanks of the Bears, "this is our last game of the season. We've waited a long time to play the Cougars again, so let's go onto that field and give it all we've got!"

"Don't worry, Coach Hanks," yelled Andrew. "This time the Bears will be on the winning side, and the Cougars will be on the losing side. No more second-place finishes for us!"

---

4. Tony and his parents had sat patiently through all the greetings and announcements on the program. Tony had hardly paid attention while the names of the second- and third-place winners were announced. Tony suddenly sat up straight, though, when he heard the president of the service club say, "And now, ladies and gentlemen, it is my honor to present the grand prize." The president paused for a moment and cleared her throat. As she made the announcement, a smile broke out on Tony's face.

---

5. Liz shifted in the saddle and looked at the time. They'd been riding for two hours. "Are we almost there?" Liz called to Aunt Fran.

"It won't be long now," said Aunt Fran encouragingly. "The ranch is just over that rise, to the left of that clump of cactuses. And there's a water tank ahead, where we can rest in the shade and have some cool water."

Unit 22

	T	F	I

1. **(A)** Michael is interested more in sports news than in political news. ☐ ☐ ☐
(B) Joe asked Michael his opinion of the president's announcement. ☐ ☐ ☐
(C) Michael said he hadn't heard about the president's announcement. ☐ ☐ ☐
(D) Michael was interested in learning how the tennis match had turned out. ☐ ☐ ☐

	T	F	I

2. **(A)** Mrs. Castillo had saved her father's life with CPR. ☐ ☐ ☐
(B) Olivia wanted to know what CPR is. ☐ ☐ ☐
(C) Olivia said that CPR is emergency treatment for someone who can't breathe. ☐ ☐ ☐
(D) Olivia likes to be prepared for emergencies. ☐ ☐ ☐

	T	F	I

3. **(A)** Andrew is on the Bears' team. ☐ ☐ ☐
(B) This is the Bears' first game of the season. ☐ ☐ ☐
(C) Andrew's team is playing in an important game. ☐ ☐ ☐
(D) Andrew told the coach not to worry. ☐ ☐ ☐

	T	F	I

4. **(A)** Tony was the winner of the grand prize. ☐ ☐ ☐
(B) The president cleared her throat before announcing the winner of the grand prize. ☐ ☐ ☐
(C) Tony's parents were at the program. ☐ ☐ ☐
(D) The second- and third-place winners were announced last. ☐ ☐ ☐

	T	F	I

5. **(A)** Aunt Fran said there was a water tank ahead. ☐ ☐ ☐
(B) The ranch is in the desert. ☐ ☐ ☐
(C) Liz was getting tired of riding. ☐ ☐ ☐
(D) Liz and Aunt Fran had been riding for ten hours. ☐ ☐ ☐

1. Mr. Nagle sighed as he looked about the huge room. There were still assorted cans of paint, two ladders, and other odds and ends that had to be put away. As he bent down to reach for the pile of dirty brushes, an idea popped into his head. *I'll leave these brushes just where they are; then tomorrow morning when Bradley comes to work, he'll find them right where he left them.*

2. "Bravo!" yelled Mr. Mirsky, as he watched Laura ride White Lightning.
    "That was the wildest ride of my life," exclaimed Laura as she dismounted. "White Lightning almost threw me off five times!"
    "I don't think that horse knew what to do with you, Laura. He just kept kicking and bucking. Maybe he thought you were glued to his back."
    The two friends roared with laughter. White Lightning was going to be an exciting horse to have around the ranch.

3. *The change had been so sudden,* Angelo thought as he stood in the wings watching the other entertainers' performances. Until last month he had been just a talkative student, clowning around for his appreciative classmates. Even Mr. Browning, his eighth-grade teacher, had found him comical. It was with Mr. Browning's encouragement that Angelo had shown up for the tryouts to recite the humorous passage from an old comedy routine. And now. . . .

4. Trina walked into the bedroom she shared with her sister. Would Keisha notice her sweater? Trina hoped not. She didn't want her sister to be upset. The sweater seemed to rub against her skin. It had fit perfectly when Trina first put it on. She thought she was being responsible by washing it before she returned it.
    Keisha finally closed her book and looked up at Trina. She smiled. "How was the party?" she asked. "Did my sweater match your slacks okay?"

5. "I think I've found something here!" shouted Dr. Fader. The other workers at the dig crowded around Dr. Fader and the small mound of dirt he was carefully sifting. "This might be the first piece of ancient Incan pottery we will find at Site C," he continued. "Sites A and B certainly provided some exciting pieces."
    As the piece of pottery was carefully dusted off, Dr. Fader's assistant, Nicole Morand, suggested, "Let's get this ready for analysis, numbering, and cataloging."

Unit 23

1. (A) The room was cluttered with paint cans, brushes, and ladders.   T F I ☐ ☐ ☐
   (B) Mr. Nagle was tired of cleaning up after Bradley.   ☐ ☐ ☐
   (C) The room was very small.   ☐ ☐ ☐
   (D) Mr. Nagle cleaned the brushes.   ☐ ☐ ☐

2. (A) Mr. Mirsky watched Laura's wild ride on White Lightning.   T F I ☐ ☐ ☐
   (B) Laura is an expert rider.   ☐ ☐ ☐
   (C) White Lightning almost threw Laura off.   ☐ ☐ ☐
   (D) Laura had never ridden before.   ☐ ☐ ☐

3. (A) Angelo was about to perform a comedy routine in a school show.   T F I ☐ ☐ ☐
   (B) Angelo was a quiet student.   ☐ ☐ ☐
   (C) Angelo was the only entertainer in the show.   ☐ ☐ ☐
   (D) Mr. Browning had encouraged Angelo to try out.   ☐ ☐ ☐

4. (A) Trina was wearing her mom's shirt.   T F I ☐ ☐ ☐
   (B) The sweater was the wrong color.   ☐ ☐ ☐
   (C) Trina worried that Keisha would notice the sweater.   ☐ ☐ ☐
   (D) Trina washed the sweater, and it shrank.   ☐ ☐ ☐

5. (A) Dr. Fader had already dug at Sites A and B.   T F I ☐ ☐ ☐
   (B) Dr. Fader thought what he found was a piece of ancient Incan pottery.   ☐ ☐ ☐
   (C) Dr. Fader found nothing at Sites A and B.   ☐ ☐ ☐
   (D) Nicole Morand was Dr. Fader's supervisor.   ☐ ☐ ☐

1.   "Here's another one, dear," said Miko's mother as she handed her daughter a card with a comical drawing on the front.

"Oh, this one is from Ms. Morales, the school's chorus director," rasped Miko. "I never thought I'd be looking forward to chorus practice so much," moaned the girl as she pulled up the covers and stared out the window longingly.

---

2.   Mr. Kelly gave an interesting assignment yesterday. Each student had to find ten articles of clothing at home and check the tags to see where the items were made. They compared their findings at school and looked on a map to locate each country. Then they talked about global trade. More items were made in the United States than people predicted, but at least two thirds were made in other countries.

---

3.   The magazine article nicknamed Mr. Rasche "Fast Eddie." At the age of 101, he had 'run' 100 yards in two minutes and forty-one seconds. (The world 100-yard record time for any age is less than ten seconds.) Mr. Rasche claimed he had set a world record for the 100-year-plus age group.

---

4.   "Let's see how close we can get to that deer before it runs away," said Olivia. "Move carefully so we get a good photograph."

"We'll stay downwind from the deer," said Alexis. "Deer have a keen sense of smell, and the wind can carry our scent to it. Then it will run even before it sees us."

The two girls moved until they were near enough to get a good picture. Olivia slowly raised her camera, focused, and pressed the button. As the shutter clicked, the deer looked up and saw them. The animal froze for an instant, then bounded off into the forest.

---

5.   The marine biologists had to work quickly because of the tide. The particular mollusk they were studying lived only in dark places, and they needed more samples to study. The cave opening was tight, and there was little head room. As they worked quickly, they began to get anxious as the incoming water rushed past their thighs. Just a few more mollusks and they would have what they needed.

		T	F	I
1.	**(A)** Miko's mother brought Miko a bouquet of flowers.	☐	☐	☐
	(B) Miko was part of a school chorus.	☐	☐	☐
	(C) Ms. Morales was Miko's aunt.	☐	☐	☐
	(D) Miko was anxious to be well again.	☐	☐	☐

		T	F	I
2.	**(A)** Mr. Kelly is a social studies teacher.	☐	☐	☐
	(B) Mr. Kelly's students had to find out where toys were made.	☐	☐	☐
	(C) The students used a map to locate where clothing items were made.	☐	☐	☐
	(D) Most of the items were made in the United States.	☐	☐	☐

		T	F	I
3.	**(A)** Mr. Rasche has been written about in a magazine.	☐	☐	☐
	(B) At the age of 100, Mr. Rasche ran 101 yards.	☐	☐	☐
	(C) Mr. Rasche's "run" was actually a walk.	☐	☐	☐
	(D) Mr. Rasche was called "Fast Eddie."	☐	☐	☐

		T	F	I
4.	**(A)** Alexis knows more about nature and the outdoors than Olivia.	☐	☐	☐
	(B) Olivia was close enough to get a good picture of the deer.	☐	☐	☐
	(C) The deer never saw the two girls.	☐	☐	☐
	(D) Deer are wary of humans.	☐	☐	☐

		T	F	I
5.	**(A)** The marine biologists specialized in sea caves.	☐	☐	☐
	(B) The researchers risked being trapped in the cave during high tide.	☐	☐	☐
	(C) The cave was beginning to crumble over their heads.	☐	☐	☐
	(D) The mollusk they were researching lives in dark habitats.	☐	☐	☐

1.   Have you ever heard of slime molds? They may sound like science fiction, but they are actually a unique type of life-form. Starting as spores that sprout only in damp environments, slime molds reproduce like fungi, live through a plantlike phase, and move in surprising ways—similar to simple animals seeking food. They appear in interesting colors and shapes that resemble orange pretzels, bright pink bubbles, and blue blobs.

2.   It had snowed heavily all winter, and last night's snowstorm had added another foot to the big pile. Making it back to camp would take time, but Mr. Craig knew he could find his way by following the path of the creek. He listened for the sound of running water and watched carefully where he placed his feet. Although Mr. Craig knew the creek was frozen solid, he also knew that the springs that gushed from the mountainside could form dangerous pools under the newly fallen snow.

3.   By working hard all year, the sixth-grade class from Parkway School had managed to earn enough money for a trip to Washington, D.C. One of the highlights of the trip was a visit to the Exhibition Hall of the National Archives, where they saw three historic documents—the Articles of Confederation, the Declaration of Independence, and the Constitution. The guide explained that the documents are sealed in bronze and glass cases filled with helium to protect them from touch, light, heat, dust, and moisture. The guide also pointed out that at a moment's notice they can be lowered into a large safe that is bombproof, shockproof, and fireproof.

4.   The ape's antics had drawn a large crowd of zoo visitors. One minute it was swinging from the trapeze; the next, it stood on its head or rolled somersaults. After showing off its gymnastic accomplishments, the ape would spread its lips in a wide grin and clap its hands, as if inviting applause. When the crowd of onlookers laughed, the ape reached through the bars of the cage and waved to many members of its appreciative audience.

5.   Seventeen-year-old Ben Franklin pulled a sheet of paper from the printing press and wiped his ink-stained hands on his leather apron. As he did this, he thought with despair, *That's all I am, a leather apron.* "Leather aprons" were what many working people were called in the 1700s. Ben was an eager reader and a budding inventor, but if he continued working here, all he would ever be was a "leather apron." He removed his apron and left Boston for Philadelphia.

Unit 25

		T	**F**	**I**

1. **(A)** Some slime molds look like pretzels and bubbles. ☐ ☐ ☐
(B) Slime molds appear only in science fiction. ☐ ☐ ☐
(C) Because they move toward food, slime molds are classified as animals. ☐ ☐ ☐
(D) Slime mold spores will not sprout in a dry environment. ☐ ☐ ☐

T F I

2. **(A)** It would be quick and easy for Mr. Craig to get back to camp. ☐ ☐ ☐
(B) There had been much winter snow. ☐ ☐ ☐
(C) The creek ran close to the campsite. ☐ ☐ ☐
(D) Mr. Craig had spent previous winters in the mountains. ☐ ☐ ☐

T F I

3. **(A)** The government considers these three documents to be very valuable. ☐ ☐ ☐
(B) The sixth-grade students had earned enough money for their Washington, D.C., trip. ☐ ☐ ☐
(C) The students were from Parkway School. ☐ ☐ ☐
(D) The bronze and glass cases are filled with hydrogen. ☐ ☐ ☐

T F I

4. **(A)** The ape had not learned to clap. ☐ ☐ ☐
(B) The ape performed gymnastic exercises. ☐ ☐ ☐
(C) Zoo visitors ignored the ape. ☐ ☐ ☐
(D) The ape enjoyed performing. ☐ ☐ ☐

T F I

5. **(A)** Ben was 18 years old. ☐ ☐ ☐
(B) Ben was convinced that Philadelphia would offer him more opportunity. ☐ ☐ ☐
(C) Ben Franklin disliked reading. ☐ ☐ ☐
(D) Ben Franklin didn't want to be a "leather apron." ☐ ☐ ☐

Ryahd purchased one ticket after another. He couldn't believe it was that difficult to throw a softball into a basket. Yet toss after toss ended up bouncing out. He finally gave up when he couldn't buy any more tickets. Then when his friend Daniel wanted him to ride with him on the Zip the Loop, Ryahd ended up having to stand and watch. At next year's fair, he planned to have a different strategy.

A. Exercising Your Skill

You can tell from the details in the passage above that the main character is a boy at a fair. Not all story characters are human, however. In a fantasy or a science-fiction story, the character might be an animal or even an object. Also, clues that identify characters are not always as clear as those in this passage. Read the following words in quotes, and then try to decide which of the characters might have said those words.

"From this high in the air, Earth seems to drift away."

a. a person in a helicopter

b. a bird

c. an astronaut

d. a kite

Did you decide that any one of the four characters could have made the statement? Now read the statement with some clues added. Is the speaker clearer now?

"From this high in the air, Earth seems to drift away. You made a really smooth takeoff in this helicopter, Grandpa!"

On your paper, write two or three types of characters that could say each of the sentences below. Remember that characters can be people, animals, or things. Use your imagination!

1. "I dove headfirst through each wave, catching brief glimpses of the distant shore."

2. "Moving farther back into the dark safety of the cave, I hoped to avoid being seen by the stranger outside."

3. "The tree limb provided security for the time being, but I knew that I would have to move on soon."

B. Expanding Your Skill

Choose two of the statements above. Rewrite them on your paper, adding a sentence or two that make the speaker easier to identify.

C. Exploring Language

Read the passages below. Decide who or what the speaker might be. On your paper, write the probable speaker of each passage. Then write the clues that helped you make that choice.

1. As I slid across the hot desert sand, I thought to myself, *I am a most fortunate creature. My wonderful scaly skin moves so smoothly across the land, yet it protects me from the sharp juts and hot surfaces of my world. How lucky I am!*

2. "There is nothing quite as exciting as shooting straight up out of the water, twisting in the air, and heading down again to the cool depths. Perhaps when they figure out the key to our language, we will tell them just how much fun it really is."

3. "WRRANGK. WRRANGK. If only I had been tuned up on schedule, I wouldn't be having all this trouble getting started! Oh, no! He's going to wear down my battery trying to start me!"

Now write a passage of your own. Give at least two clues about the character that could be speaking. Read your passage aloud, and ask your classmates to guess who or what the character is.

D. Expressing Yourself

Choose one of these activities.

1. Write a retelling of a popular fable or folktale. Tell the story from the point of view of one of the minor characters—or from the point of view of an animal or an object in the story. You might, for example, retell the story of *Cinderella* from the point of view of one of the horses, or of the glass slipper. Share your story with classmates, and have them guess who or what is telling the story.

2. With some classmates, make up a skit that could be from a popular television cartoon or situation comedy. Make sure there are enough clues in the conversation to allow your audience to guess who or what each of the characters is.